1. CLIFTON

Explore Bristol

ON FOOT

EXPLOREWALKS UK

Julia Killingback and Michael Pascoe

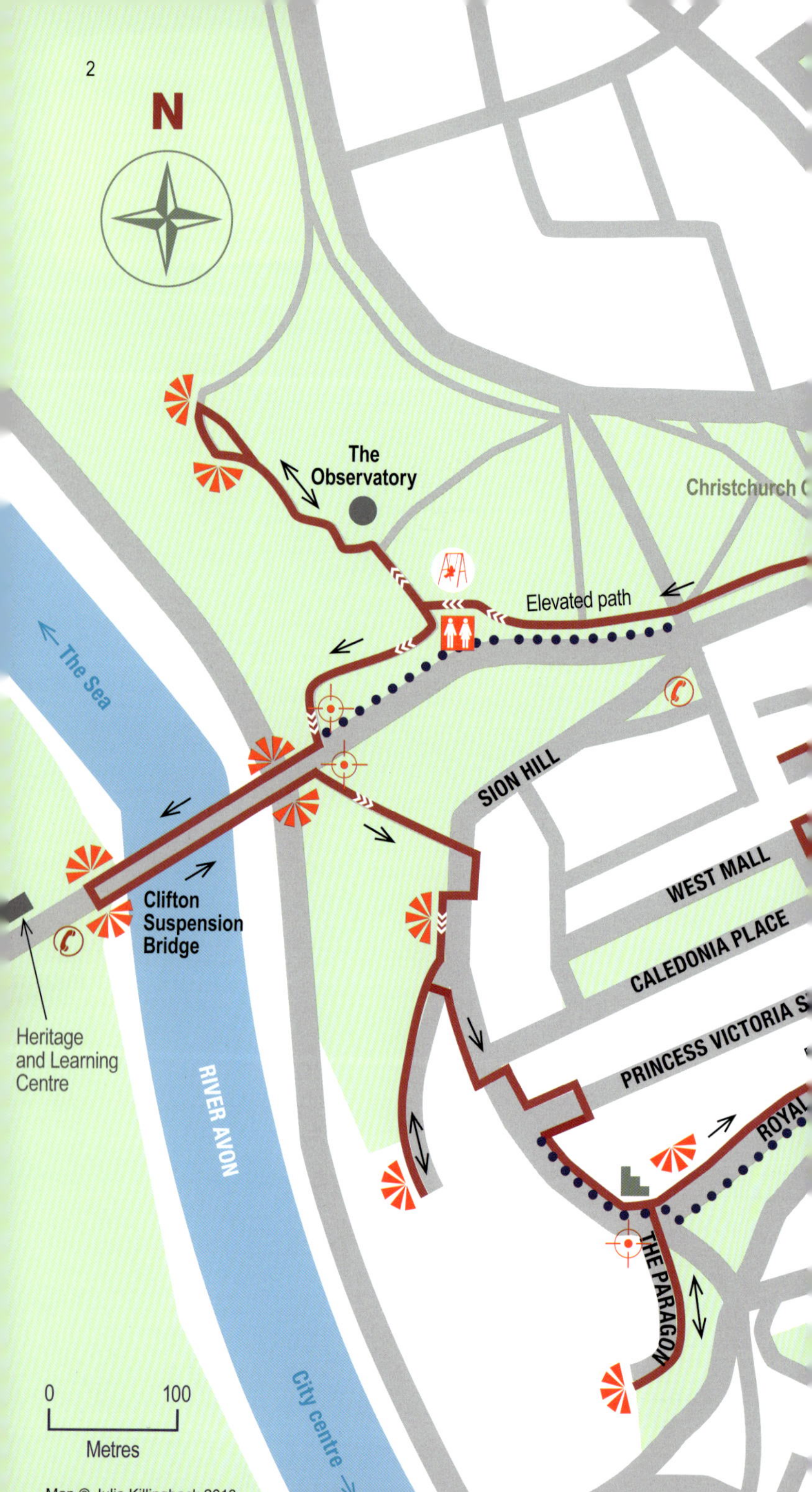
N
The Observatory
Christchurch G
Elevated path
The Sea
SION HILL
WEST MALL
CALEDONIA PLACE
PRINCESS VICTORIA ST
ROYAL
THE PARAGON
Clifton
Suspension
Bridge
Heritage
and Learning
Centre
RIVER AVON
City centre
0
100
Metres

1. CLIFTON

Explore Bristol

EXPLOREWALKS UK

ON FOOT

ARCH
HOUSE
DELI

A Circular Walk around the heart of historic Clifton

The walk is mainly on the level, but alternative routes have been indicated where mobility is an issue.

Full Circular Walk

Total distance approx. 2¾ miles / 4.5 kms
Average time needed – 2¼ hours

Shortened Walk

Total distance approx. 2¼ miles / 3.6 kms
Average time needed – 1¾ hours

Our walk description begins at the Clifton Village Bus Stop

See the map pages 2 and 3.
This stop is close to the junction of Boyce's Avenue with Clifton Down Road, near the pedestrian crossing.
OS Explorer map 154, Sat Nav: Postcode BS8 4AF

Get there

By bus – From Temple Meads Station
– From Bristol City Centre
– From Bristol Bus Station (a nearby stop)
Ask for the Clifton Village Bus Stop.

By Open Top Bus This makes a circular tour of Bristol (from February to December). It stops at the Clifton Village stop. Seasonal information: www.citysightseeingbristol.co.uk

By taxi – ask to be set down near the Clifton Village Bus Stop in Clifton Down Road.

Please note
This is a circular walk, so you may choose to begin at any point on our route knowing that you will return to the same spot eventually.

Mobility Impaired Information There are some steps and two slopes on this route. If you wish to avoid these, just look for our suggested **Options**. There are alternative routes marked on the map.

THE QUIZ Look for the questions within the text. Then STOP! (You should be able to discover the answer from this spot.) When you think you know it, turn over– the numbered answers are shown at the bottom of the NEXT page. GOOD LUCK!

FUN FACTS. Look out for the smiley face telling you more as you go along.

Welcome to Clifton

Until the mid-1700s there were few inhabitants of Clifton on the hill. Sheep were grazed on the downland and market gardens supplied food to nearby Bristol. There were some farmhouses and a handful of mansions, built by wealthy Bristol merchants anxious to escape the stench and the noise of the overcrowded city below. The riverside Hotwell spa in the Avon Gorge close by attracted thousands of visitors in the eighteenth century.

In the 1780s there was a national building boom and it was then that many of Clifton's fine terraces were laid out. However, in 1793 Britain went to war with Revolutionary France. A building slump followed and many of the terraces were not completed until two decades later. During the nineteenth century many of these terraces became lodging houses for visitors wishing to view the beautiful scenery, visit Clifton Suspension Bridge or take the waters at the Hotwell spa. In Victorian times, especially from the 1850s onwards, the area expanded to the east and newly-built villas became home to the cultured and leisured classes, helped by the establishment of two Assembly Rooms, two independent schools and a university college – later to become the University of Bristol. By the end of the century virtually the whole area of Clifton was built up.

▲ Proposals for the development of Clifton c.1787 James Blackamore

The first half of the twentieth century brought much change to Clifton. The coming of the motor car, smaller families and fewer servants meant that the wealthy could move further afield to rural areas and live in more manageable houses. This resulted in many larger Clifton houses being converted into flats, now comprising the majority of its buildings.

In the second half of the century post-war shortages of building materials and absentee landlords caused the deterioration of many historic properties. However, from around the 1960s Georgian houses, often sold comparatively cheaply, were appreciated by their new and caring owners who frequently did much of the restoration themselves. In 1974 Clifton was declared a Conservation Area. Towards the end of the century, as elsewhere, many local service shops gave way to restaurants, estate agents and boutiques.

Jane Austen *(1775-1817)* was for a while a resident of Clifton, where is not known. While staying here she wrote to her sister Cassandra, *It is two years tomorrow since we left Bath for Clifton, with what happy feelings of escape.* She was not alone in her love of Clifton – it remains a popular place to live.

THE WALK

Facing the Clifton Village bus stop, go left to cross **Boyce's Avenue** and then, using the pedestrian crossing, **Clifton Down Road**. Walk down the right-hand side of **Princess Victoria Street**. After the corner pub, the first shop on your right has a decorated Victorian façade, as does another pub, further down on your left. Beyond this on your left is the *Clifton Library* dating from 1852. ● **Question 1** *(Look at the bottom of the page.)*

Clifton library

➔ Continue, passing Waterloo Street on your right. Pause when you reach the junction with the **Mall**. Look left at the ornate Edwardian Baroque façade, constructed in 1906 for a building firm. The beautiful doors reflect the decoration of the ironwork above. In Georgian times on the same site there were large stables used by the nearby Assembly Rooms. Look down the lower part of Princess Victoria Street, originally individual stables and coach houses serving the nearby terraced houses of the wealthy. Later these small buildings were turned into garages and then into charming mews houses. There is some modern in-filling.

➔ Keeping on the same side, turn right and walk up the Mall. **Caledonia Place** and the *Mall Gardens* come into view. Look at the bank of 1922 on the opposite corner. Its pediment reflects the design of a former Georgian house here.

➔ Cross the road and stop outside its portico. Inside, the bank still retains its impressive banking hall. Note the two unusual lamp standards on either side of the gardens in the Mall bearing the city's coat of arms. They date from 1893 and were amongst the first experimental electric street lights in Bristol. From Bristol's first gas company in 1816 until the end of the century this was the only form of street lighting. In several streets residents have fought to retain the original lamp standards and gas lighting – an important feature of Clifton's historic past.

➔ Leaving the bank, cross Caledonia Place to the cobbled paving at the top of the gardens.

● **Question 1**

Look up! Read the words. What once went on here?

TURN OVER FOR ANSWERS

▲ **The Assembly Rooms**
Completed 1811
Francis Howard Greenway
Architect

Look up at the magnificent façade of the *Assembly Rooms* opposite, built 1806-11. It is now a private club. The building has six Ionic columns and a fine pediment displaying the coat of arms of its Huguenot developer, John Auriol. If you have the chance, return at night to see it floodlit. The architect was Francis Howard Greenway *(1777-1837)*. In 1812 he was convicted of forgery for which he was transported to Australia. There, he was employed by Governor Macquarie *(1761-1824)* and designed over 40 buildings in the Sydney area. As a result he is regarded as the father of Australian architecture.

Imagine a little girl aged 11 looking out from the first-floor windows of the Assembly Rooms. She would have looked down over the garden close to you where lots of people had come to cheer her. The year was 1830 and the little girl was visiting Clifton with her mother. The building was a hotel at the time. ● **Question 2**

● Question 2

Look at the picture of the little girl. Who do you think she was?

Did you know?

For many years, the head of Bristolian forger Francis Greenway appeared on Australian banknotes!

The Cloakroom, Clifton Assembly Rooms, 1817 ▲
Detail from an oil painting by Rolinda Sharples *1793-1838*

Rolinda Sharples, a Bristol-born painter, specialized in portraits and genre paintings in oil. This is one of only a few Georgian paintings existing today that depicts assemblies. It shows a happy group in the cloakroom preparing for an entertaining evening.

Turn to look down the *Mall Gardens.* This is one of the finest of no fewer than 35 communal gardens in Clifton and Hotwells. They solved the problem of supplying every terraced house with access to what in the eighteenth century were called *pleasure grounds* for all the surrounding residents to enjoy. Immediately in front of you, in summer, is a display of *Lychnis chalcedonica*, known locally as the *Flower of Bristol.* It is possible that it was first brought to England as a garden plant at the time of the Crusades, but it could have been introduced in the Middle Ages. It was so named because Bristol once manufactured a bright red cloth of the same colour as the flower. The colour is now used for the hoods of the University of Bristol's graduate gowns.

➔ Return to the bank and walk down the wide pavement of Caledonia Place. The nearer ends of these two grand parallel terraces were built in the 1780s. Note the Georgian cast-iron door knockers and the iron railings. Number 40 has an unusual knocker in the form of a hand-held laurel wreath.

The decorated electric lamp standards of 1905 also bear Bristol's coat of arms.

Look at Number 37. The windows above the doors are called fanlights. They look like the fans ladies used in Georgian times. Look out for the many different patterns of these windows on your walk.

➔ Stop on the pavement once you reach the first road between the two gardens. Pause here to look on down Caledonia Place. All these houses, mainly built in the 1840s, have balconies.

There are 24 stone blocks beside the road. Before cars were invented people used horse-drawn carriages. These blocks were steps to help people to climb up into them more easily.

Answer 1

CHRISTCHURCH SCHOOLS – once a primary school. The boys went to their lessons through one door – the girls through the other.

Answer 2

She was the young Princess Victoria. Her mother brought her to Clifton so that people could see their future queen.

Life in a Georgian terraced household

While here, you might like to read this brief note about life in a Georgian household:

The ground floor housed the dining room and an everyday sitting room. The first floor was the finest and contained a magnificent drawing room and an adjoining music room. Many of the ground and first floors still have their original large folding doors between the front and back rooms. This enabled the two rooms to be used separately as a sitting room and a bedroom for lodgers, or to be turned into one huge room for larger social events. The family bedrooms were on the second floor and the nurseries and servants inhabited the attic. The basements of each house were taken up with the servants' quarters and a kitchen. Other servants and local tradesmen lived in small two-storey houses behind the grand terraces. A few included stables but most families hired carriages from nearby livery yards.

Most lavatories were earth closets in the garden, emptied by a *night-soil man* who sold the contents as manure to local market gardeners – an early eco-friendly idea. Once mains water became available in the middle of the nineteenth century, bathrooms were added to the backs of the houses. Rainwater down pipes were hidden at the rear. ● **Question 3**

The pleasing design of Georgian sash windows, with their small panes of glass, was dictated by the largest size of glass which could be manufactured at the time. Today you can see that some windows have larger panes. These were produced later in the nineteenth century when glass manufacturing techniques improved. Many houses retain their original internal wooden window shutters – good for security and really good for helping keep the houses warm. The iron squares in the pavement cover coal chutes. Coal was brought by horse and cart and dropped down these into the cellars below for storage. Before central heating existed, each room had its individual fireplace. The long rows of chimney pots, often eight or ten to a house, add to Clifton's distinctive character.

● **Question 3**

Before piped water, life wasn't so easy. How do you think people got the water they needed for cooking and washing?

A Georgian house, Harley Place

Assembly Rooms

Corner house West Mall

Carters Buildings

➔ Now take the short road between the upper and lower gardens. These were originally planted with two rows of Holm Oaks, a favourite in noblemen's gardens.

➔ Walk towards the red pillar box opposite.

● **Question 4**

➔ Walk right, along the local pennant stone pavement of West Mall, leaving the gardens to your right.

You are now in **West Mall**. Look up at nearby Number 7 with its pediment. This will give you a clue that originally the plan was to build a square around this top garden. Each central and "corner" house was to have a pediment. Five of them still exist, but the side meant to face the Assembly Rooms was never built. Fifty years later the terrace was extended down the slope.

Look up at Number 5. Can you see a badge (fire-mark) on the wall? Today, if there is a fire anyone can call the fire service to put it out. In the old days, people couldn't get help unless they showed a fire-mark on their house. They had to pay money to an insurance company to buy one. This fire-mark is for the Westminster insurance company. If there was a fire the insurance company would send its own horse-drawn fire engine. Imagine poor horses galloping along, pulling a heavy fire pump, filled with water and carrying the brave firemen to the scene of a fire!

The corner building once housed a chemist's shop established as early as 1832. There is a magnificent painted ceiling and some of the original chemist's shop fittings are still inside.

● **Question 5**

➔ Turn left up the Mall.

Look at the carved wooden window moulding around the first window on your left. Above the side door notice that the windows are not all genuine. None are real except the

Answer 3

Rainwater from the roof flowed down drainpipes into a tank in the cellar. When someone upstairs called for hot water, maids heated it on a hot stove in the basement kitchen. Imagine them having to carry heavy jugs full of steaming water up all those stairs!

▲ **West Mall**
The earlier houses
– built 1780s-1811
John Eveleigh of Bath
Architect

first-floor right-hand one – the others are painted to resemble real windows. Often this was done to improve the look of the buildings making them appear more regular and balanced. However, between 1696 and 1851 the government imposed a tax on houses with more than ten windows so many poorer owners blocked some up to save money. Perhaps this gave rise to the expression *daylight robbery!* There were also taxes on men servants, riding horses and powder for men's wigs!

➔ At the junction with **Portland Street** turn left into it. You will pass *James Place,* then *Carter's Buildings.* These were nineteenth-century working-class houses around courtyards. The larger building with a tall door and two-storey-high windows was once the parish hall of local Christ Church.

At the end of the street is the *Coronation Tap,* a popular cider pub. (Neighbouring Somerset is renowned for its apple orchards producing strong brews.) The pub was previously a seventeenth-century farmhouse and is one of the oldest buildings in Clifton.

▼ **Coronation Tap**

Question 4

Look at the letters on the post box. What does the V stand for? Think of a famous queen ...

Question 5

Pause to look across the road at the two shops to the left of the big Assembly Rooms. What creatures can you see carved in the woodwork?

Victorian Christ Church

➔ Retrace your steps. Stop at the junction of the Mall and Portland Street. The corner building here on your left has an *Art Nouveau* bracket for a sign from about 1890.

➔ Cross the Mall diagonally to the opposite corner.

Look at the edge of the pavement. It's made of cast iron. This was put here long before the days of cars to stop the iron-bound wheels of passing carriages and carts from cutting into the softer stone kerbs. There are lots of these edgings in Bristol. Look out for more on your walks.

➔ Walk up the Mall on the right-hand pavement. You will pass Gloucester Street on your left, still with its original hand-cut cobbles. The cobbles are made of Cornish granite because local stone was too soft. They were laid in Georgian times before Bristol Roads Surveyor John Loudon Macadam *(1756-1836)* pioneered a new and successful method of road building. Tarmac was named after him.

Draper's monuments

➔ At the top of the Mall, use the pedestrian crossing to *Christchurch Green.* Pause (with your back to the crossing) at the meeting point of the five paths. Across the grass to your right you can see a sarcophagus which is one of the earliest war memorials in Britain. It was erected by General Sir William Draper *(1721-1787)* who lived nearby. The memorial commemorates his officers killed during the Seven Years War *(1756-1763)*. This was the war in which Britain captured India and North America from the French. Britain also seized the Philippine Islands in the Pacific Ocean from the Spanish. Note the tall obelisk, also erected by Draper. It honours Prime Minister William Pitt the Elder *(1708-1788)*.

The diagonal path to the right leads the eye to the splendid Victorian *Christ Church,* opened in 1841. Its tall spire is a dominant local landmark.

Left of this, across the Green and beyond the trees, you

Answer 4

***VR* are the first letters of the Latin words *Victoria Regina*, meaning *Queen Victoria*. She reigned from 1837 to 1901.**

Answer 5

Dolphins. They are having a swimming time

▲**Clifton Down Hotel**
Formerly the Bath Hotel
Completed 1865

may glimpse a fine terrace, Harley Place, begun in 1788. (See picture page 13.) The entire Green is lit by a series of former gas lamps, now converted to electricity. The Green looks very romantic after dark when the lamps are lit.

➔ Now walk left, along the pavement bordering Clifton Green. You will pass **Gloucester Row** on your left. Cross Observatory Road. You reach the decorative cast-iron Victorian fountain (*right*) with its Biblical inscriptions. You will see Bristol's coat of arms and its motto: *Virtute et industria* which loosely translates from Latin as: *By brain and brawn.* There is an information board. Look downhill at the building with the large portico in Sion Place. Now luxury flats this was once a hotel. Isambard Kingdom Brunel *(1806-1859)* the designer of the nearby *Clifton Suspension Bridge,* stayed in the original hotel when celebrating the laying of the foundation stone of his bridge on 27 August 1836 – a magnificent event.

You can imagine Mr Brunel in his tall hat striding out across the Green to give orders to his workmen busy building the two huge towers of the new bridge.

Bristol's biggest surprise is Clifton.
Sir John Betjeman *(1906-1984)*

The walk now goes uphill to the *Observatory*, giving amazing views of the *Suspension Bridge* and the *Gorge*. (You will come to the bridge later.)

Option

Should you wish to avoid a climb and a few shallow steps, continue on the flat (with the road to your left) towards the Suspension Bridge.

Meeting Point – *Suspension Bridge* – *right-hand tollhouse.*

➔**The circular route continues.** Take the higher path close to the edge of Clifton Green. Quite soon you will suddenly find yourself looking straight down the centre line of the bridge. At one point you will see the far tower through the arch of the nearer one.

Children. If there is time, have fun in the playground to your right – don't forget to have a go on the small natural rock slide on the far side.

➔ Continue to climb the path.

The views of the bridge become more and more dramatic. Below the hilltop, on your left, is another limestone rockslide, worn shiny by generations of enthusiastic sliders! Some locals call it the Donkey Slide because donkeys were used when early quarrying was carried out here. Ahead of you is the round tower of the *Observatory*. (We walk to this later.)

➔ Our route goes left, past the top of the slide, along the cliff-edge path. You are about to see one of Bristol's most famous and breathtaking views of the bridge as it crosses the *Avon Gorge*. It hangs 75 metres (245 feet) above river level at high tide. The panoramic view over the city of Bristol, and North Somerset to your right, is magnificent. To the right of the bridge you can see an imitation Swiss chalet built by another Victorian civil engineer, Francis Cox, who had worked for some time in Switzerland.

'You climb the hills by steps and look back on a forest of towers, spires and masts of vessels that have threaded up the Avon Gorge to reach the Port of Bristol.'

Sir John Betjeman *(1906-1984)*

Below you runs the *River Avon.* At low tide the river looks like a miserable stream, trickling between mud banks. There is a 12 metre (36 feet) rise and fall of tide here. (Nearby Avonmouth has the second highest to lowest tide difference in the world after that in the Bay of Fundy off Nova Scotia, Canada.)

▲ **The river Avon from Observatory Hill** detail from a panorama by Thomas Rowbotham *c.*1830

Bristol lies 9.5 kilometres (6 miles) from the Bristol Channel. This meant that, a thousand years ago, the river provided the inland port with good protection from invaders. The winding river and huge tidal range presented a major navigational challenge in the days of sail. Vessels could only reach the city docks during the limited hours of a high tide and leave only on an ebb tide. The fickle winds, owing to the high cliffs of the gorge, meant that large sailing ships needed to be carefully towed along the twisting river. The ships' bows were steered in the right direction by *hobblers* – up to ten strong men manning three or four large rowing boats. (*See right*)

▼ Detail from etching by Nicholas Pocock *c.*1786

The Pirates of Pill

Ships approaching Bristol had to pay pilots from the village of Pill to guide them up and down the river. Fees were high because the job was skilled and cargoes valuable. Some ship's owners thought the charges too high and called pilots the *'Pirates of Pill'.*

The Giant's cave

➔ Our walk continues a short way along the cliff-edge path. You will pass a display board which describes the interesting wildlife of the Avon Gorge. The path curves towards the gorge. You then reach another amazing viewpoint. Continue along. On a bank nearby is another display board facing the winding gorge. It shows a painting of the scene as it was in 1825. The work is by Samuel Jackson *(1794-1869)*, a member of the Bristol School of Artists. ● **Question 6** On a clear day you can see the Welsh hills beyond the Bristol Channel from here.

➔ Now take the upper path back towards the Observatory. The grassy cliff top area surrounding it was once an Iron Age camp of about 350 BC which controlled an ancient ford crossing the river 100 metres (320 feet) below. (See the notice board about Clifton Camp.)

The *Observatory* was originally a windmill, re-built in the 1820s, after being damaged by a fire. William West *(1801-1861)*, an artist and amateur astronomer, installed a Victorian *camera obscura* in the building. Through a revolving lens on the roof a 360-degree image of the entire surroundings is projected, in a darkened room at the top of the tower, on to a large white-painted concave dish in a seemingly magical way.

Hey! Do you want to be a Spy in the Sky? If you visit the *camera obscura* you will be able to see everything that is going on around the tower right now in all directions. Perhaps you will spot friends who will have no idea that you are spying on them.

Probably from curiosity, West also dug a steep tunnel through the cliff from the *Observatory* down to a natural cave, known as the *Giant's Cave* in the side of the gorge. Both the *Observatory* and the cave are often open to the public. If you don't mind steps, first climb the tower and then go down the tunnel to enjoy a dramatic cliff-side view from the cave.

Clifton Rocks

Millions of years ago the limestone rocks of the Avon Gorge were formed from sediments on the sea bed. Sea creatures added to the layers. The sediment hardened into layers and were tilted by movements of the earth's crust to the angles we see today.

▲ The Avon Gorge at Sunset c.1825. Watercolour by Samuel Jackson

Look out! You might meet Giant Vincent in his cave. He was supposed to have lived and roamed here long before there was a gorge.

The story goes that two giant brothers, Vincent and Goram (who lived over in Blaise, near Bristol), both fell in love with a beautiful girl from Avonmouth down by the sea. She was called *Avonia.* Avonia decided to find out who was the stronger. She agreed to marry the first brother to reach her. They would only get there by digging a deep channel. This would drain a nearby lake.

Giant Goram slowly got to work. He dug a small valley through Blaise. He was lazy, stopped for a beer and soon fell fast asleep. But Clifton's Giant Vincent worked very hard. He grabbed his pickaxe and quickly dug out the whole of the Avon Gorge. Vincent was first to reach Avonia. The lake drained into the newly dug valley and the *River Avon* has flowed through the gorge ever since.

At last lazy Goram woke up. When he heard he had lost the competition he was very cross. He stamped his foot in a rage. If you go to Blaise today you can still see that giant footprint pressed deep into the rock. It was too late – Vincent and Avonia were already happily married.

Question 6

Look at Samuel Jackson's beautiful painting. How many ships did he see out on the water that day?

➔ Leaving the *Observatory*, take the path around to the left. A notice board here describes Clifton Camp. Turn right downhill to retrace part of the route you came up. Go past the slide and take the first footpath to the right. It comes out close to the Suspension Bridge right-hand tollhouse.

Meeting Point – right-hand tollhouse.

There are public toilets nearby.

Option *For those not wishing to cross the bridge, cross the road with care.*

Meeting Point – left-hand tollhouse.

Bristol whitebeam

➔ **Continuing the Circular Walk** – right-hand footpath. (This includes the **Clifton Suspension Bridge Heritage and Learning Centre** and shop on the Somerset side.)The bridge is free for pedestrians. Go through the entrance and pause to read on.

This impressive structure was designed by Isambard Kingdom Brunel in 1830, when he was just 23. Brunel called his design *my first child, my darling*. It was only partly built in his lifetime because funds ran out. It was completed in 1864 as a memorial to him. Designed for horse traffic, it now carries over four million vehicles a year. Brunel would have been astonished!

Bristol onion

➔ Walk on towards the towers. In a small garden on your right you will see information describing some of the 35 rare wild plants which grow on the cliffs of the *Avon Gorge*. Two kinds of Whitebeam trees, the Bristol rock cress and the *Bristol onion* are unique to it. The cliffs of the gorge are home to peregrine falcons and kestrels.

Just beyond the tower look for the gap in the path where it turns on to the bridge. Straddle it! You can now feel what it's like to have one foot on firm ground, the other on a suspended bridge. This moves when cars go by. As metal expands in hot weather and contracts in cold, these gaps are vital to stop the bridge getting damaged.

Answer 6

He saw five boats out on the water. (The other boat was just a stick-in-the-mud!)

Now look back at the *Giant's Cave* in the cliff face below the *Observatory.* You will see just how adventurous you were if you visited it! You may even see some skillful rock climbers carefully inching their way up the steep cliffs.

▲ **The New Bridge**
Spring 1865
Opened 8 December 1864.
(Inset) Watch for peregrine falcons here.

A Girl Racer

The first member of the public to cross the bridge on its opening day was Mary Griffiths from Hanham, Bristol. Picking up her long skirts, 21-year-old Mary, raced a young man from the Clifton side to the Leigh Woods side and beat him by a few yards.

Portrait of I. K. Brunel

▲ Maquette of Brunel by John Doubleday (b 1947)

➔ Now cross the suspended bridge. From tower to tower measures 215 metres (702 feet). **At the end you may wish to visit the Heritage Centre**. Our return is on the opposite footpath. Please cross the road with care. Look up at the inscription on the near tower – *Suspensa vix via fit*, Latin for A suspended way was made with difficulty. Vix is probably a pun on the name of local wine merchant William Vick *(1707-1754)* who originally bequeathed money to build the bridge.

➔ Walk to the parapet wall beyond the right-hand tower.

What a view! You can see a forest of hundreds of chimney pots along its skyline – no wonder the city was once so smoky. The lone house nestling on the side of the cliff opposite is called *Tuffleigh*. It was once the house of the manager of the large hotel to its right. Look further down. This riverside area is a part of Hotwells. At the left-hand end of a long elevated Georgian terrace you can see a curved building with columns. This *Colonnade* was an eighteenth-century shopping mall with lodgings above – now the only surviving part of what in the 1700s was the popular *Hotwell Spa*. Beyond, to the right of this you can see the *Cumberland Basin* – the entrance to Bristol City Docks. The huge red-brick buildings in the middle distance were built as bonded warehouses between 1905 and 1919. Tobacco, once the source of much of Bristol's wealth, was stored here until customs duty was paid. Right beneath you on this near (Somerset) side of the gorge is the railway line between Bristol and the modern Royal Portbury Dock near Portishead. Freight from vast container ships is brought inland along this line.

➔ Return across the bridge on this side.

Meeting Point – the Clifton side toll house.

➔ Leaving the tollhouse, take the path downhill across the green towards the attractive terrace of **Sion Hill**. These houses with their black-and-white canopies were built around 1780.

'Clifton is situated on the top of a hill commanding a view of Bristol and its neighbourhood, conveniently elevated above the dirt and noise of the city. Here are houses, rocks, woods, town and country in one small spot: and beneath the sweetly flowing Avon, so celebrated by the poets. Indeed, there can hardly be a more beautiful spot.' Humphrey Davy *October 1798*

➔ Carefully cross the road and walk on down the left-hand pavement, close to the fine houses which face the gorge. The pennant stone pavement has parallel grooves hand-cut into it – an eighteenth-century version of a non-slip surface. Each of these houses is different. Note the interesting door furniture. Number 8 has an original bell pull and a knocker with winged sphinxes and lotus flowers – the Egyptian style was very popular at that time.

▲ The view back towards Clifton from the Somerset side of the bridge

Look at the huge tree growing up the front of Number 7. It isn't really a tree at all but a beautiful flowering plant called Wisteria. It could be 200 years old.

The sculptor and wood engraver Gertrude Hermes *(1901-1983)* once lived at Number 5.

▲ *The Starlings*
Colour linocut 1965 by Gertrude Hermes, sculptor and wood engraver

➔ Cross the road here for a fine view of the bridge from the *Lookout*. This was sponsored by the Clifton and Hotwells Improvement Society in 1994. If you can, do return here at night to see the bridge illuminated – it is a magnificent sight.

The bench supports look like twisted branches. Called *Rustic* this design was very popular a century ago.

● **Question 7**

● **Question 7**

Look for the maker's name on a twiggy bench. What else do you think these clever metal workers made?

Victorian bathers

Below the *Lookout* the steep and winding *Zig-Zag* path goes right down to river level. It arrives at the site of the original Hotwell spa shown (left) as from Sion Hill.

➔ Now turn to face the hotel. When the spa at the foot of the cliff closed in 1872 the Hotwell spring water was piped up to a new pump room which opened here in 1894. Four years later the room became part of the *Grand Spa and Hydro* (now the *Avon Gorge Hotel*).

➔ Walk down **Prince's Lane** to the right of the railings of the *Clifton Rocks Railway.* Here there are two buildings, both highly decorated. They were designed in the 1890s for Sir George Newnes MP *(1851-1910)*. You will see ahead of you the old entrance to the baths. The words *AD BATHS 97* are carved above the door and there are wyverns (two-legged dragons) on either side. Below is the face of the mythical Green Man, looking like a sea monster. To your left is the extraordinary façade of the Pump Room. *GN* (for George Newnes) is carved above the door. It is framed by two caryatids (columns in female form). Look up if you want to see cupids! ● **Question 8** and ● **Question 9**

➔ Return up Prince's Lane and turn sharp right along Sion Hill towards the hotel. You pass the entrance to the top station of the once busy *Clifton Rocks Railway.* Pause here.

Peer through the railings. You can see the top of the old railway tunnel. Look how steep it was.

Because wealthy residents in this area didn't want noisy trams in Clifton, Newnes thought up this alternative scheme to bring people up here. His funicular railway was opened in 1893. It ran through a diagonal tunnel under the cliffs. There were four tracks, each carrying a carriage or car. Two started at the top, two at the bottom. The carriages were attached to parallel cables which hauled them up or lowered them down. The system was hydraulic, powered by

Answer 7

Some arms show the name *Bristol Wagon Works.* They made seats – and railway wagons!

● **Question 8**

What is a cupid?

the weight of water poured into a large tank beneath each carriage while it rested at the top station, until it was heavy enough to counter-balance the weight of the upcoming car and that of its passengers waiting at the bottom. The earliest fare was a penny up and a halfpenny down.

People came here to marvel at the views, picnic on the *Downs* and visit the *Zoo*. Those going down could catch a tram at river level to the city centre or take the extremely popular boat trips from the (now derelict) riverside quays to ports in Somerset, North Devon and South Wales. For many years the pubs in South Wales were closed on Sundays so a boat trip to Bristol was very welcome. The *Rocks Railway* closed in 1934 when the Portway – the road at the foot of the gorge linking Bristol to the docks at Avonmouth – was built.

During the Second World War *(1939-1945)* the tunnel was divided into a series of flat levels. Parts were used by the BBC as a bomb-proof studio and radio-transmitting station. The top section became an air-raid shelter for local residents. The site is currently being restored and the railway, although no longer operating, is sometimes open to the public – see the notices on the railings.

▲ **Top Station**
Clifton Rocks Railway
Opened 1893
Closed 1934

● **Question 9**

There are lions' heads along the edge of the roof. How many are there?

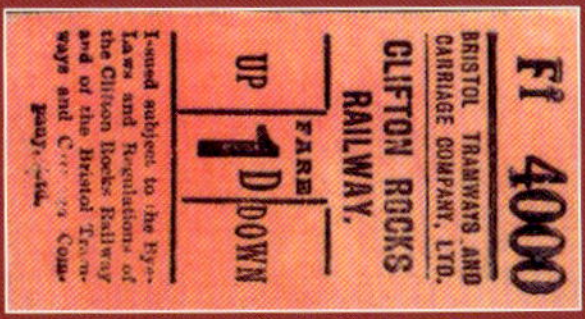

What's in a name?

Clifton:
settlement by a cliff
Old English

➔ While here, look across at the last house with its long delicate balcony. It's called *Sion Spring House.* At the end of the eighteenth century the owner of the adjacent house (at that time the final property here) dug a deep well, struck a stream of warm water similar to that down in Hotwells, and nearly killed the workmen involved. He built a new spa – *Sion Spring House.* Sadly it failed, but profit was made by piping the warm water to 400 nearby houses, an extraordinary luxury at the time.

Lower Caledonia Place

➔ Continue along. You pass the newer end of imposing Caledonia Place. To your right, below the long wall, the hotel once had a sumptuous pump room whose frontage you saw earlier. It became a cinema in the 1920s and later still, during the *Swinging Sixties,* a popular ballroom – *the* place to rock and roll on a Saturday night! Just past the plaque you will see the doorway brought here from the *original Hotwells Pump Room* at the foot of the gorge. Through this entrance once passed the illustrious eighteenth-century visitors of rank and fashion. It was re-erected up here in 1894 to commemorate 200 years of the spa. Read the centre part first, then the left side followed by the right. It reads *The Original Pump Room Erected 1694 / This Spring Was / Renowned.*

Opposite the main entrance to the hotel is *St Vincent's Priory,* an unusual Regency Gothic house of about 1828. Despite its name it was never used for religious purposes. Look up at the delightful twisting figures clinging to the building. Two sphinxes guard the entrance. Cross the road to the *Priory.* ● **Question 10**

The Priory

Now, look back at the hotel. Above the canopy, over the front door, is the monogram of the former *Grand Spa and Hydro.* Walk along to the corner. Notice the unusual stepped pavement. A Georgian carriage's folding step would rest securely on the lower kerb, making it easier for those alighting to step on to the upper pavement out of the mud. You can see a metal ring set into the pavement. Ropes used to be wound round this to help lower goods into the nearby cellars for storage.

Answer 8

Cupids are said to be the gods of love. The one with the wine glass might have a long wait before his friend with a jug fills it up. Oh dear!

Answer 9

Eight lions are watching you.

→ Turn left into **Princess Victoria Street** once bustling with stables. On your left, at Number 112, you will see a plaque to Keith Floyd *(1943-2009)* the flamboyant Bristol chef. Walk on. Cross the street to narrow Oxford Place**.** The corner house also has a plaque commemorating Berthold Lubetkin *(1901-1990)* a pioneer of modern architecture. Now, walk back towards the hotel, keeping left. Look for the last house which has a pretty fanlight and bootscraper. Look down at the kerbstones close to it.

What a surprise! They look like a jigsaw. What a brilliant idea to hold each stone in place.

The corner building with its pretty balcony was once a shop. If you can manage a few steps, continue around the corner along the high pavement of **Wellington Terrace.**

Option. *For those wishing to avoid steps, follow the lower left-hand roadside pavement.*

Meeting Point – at the foot of the lower short flight of steps at the end of the Wellington Terrace.

Question 10

What can you see (made of cast-iron) low down to the right of the door?

The Paragon

As you walk along, note the houses opposite, called *Prince's Buildings*. They were begun in 1790 by local architect William Paty *(1758-1800)*. **Question 11** You can also see the three feathers crest of the Prince of Wales and his motto *Ich Dien*, meaning *I serve*. (He later became King George IV and reigned from 1820-1830.) On reaching the short flight of steps at the end of the terrace, go down to road level.

Meeting Point – at road level.

➔ Cross the road to the entrance to the **Paragon**. This was built between 1809 and 1814. The dramatic concave terrace follows the natural curve of the cliff. Note the unusual convex porches and doors, with windows on the approach side so that the owners could see who was about to arrive. There are fine twisted railings and a variety of door furniture. The hand-carved stone gutter is unusual.

Walk to the far end of the terrace and pause by the garden railings. There is another fine view across the gorge to *Rownham Hill*. In winter, when the trees are bare, you can enjoy a splendid view past the rear of Prince's Buildings back towards the *Suspension Bridge*. The delightful terraced gardens appear to tumble right down the side of the gorge. Retrace your steps to the main road. Note the fine *Holm Oak* as you leave.

➔ Cross the road again to the base of the two flights of steps opposite. These lead up to **Royal York Crescent**. While here at road level, pause to look up at the two stern Georgian instructions *Stick No Bills* carved in the concave wall and again higher up the steps. Like us, the Georgians stuck flyers, or bills, where they shouldn't – fly posting isn't new!

Option – Lower route Royal York Crescent (Avoiding steps.) Cross the road towards the large stone pillar. Pause here to read the **Royal York Crescent description** (on page 32) if you would like to get a flavour of this remarkable eighteenth-century development. Continue along the right-hand pavement parallel to the terrace above. Cross to the left where the pavement ends. Continue to **Regent Street**.

Answer 10

It is a bootscraper. Long ago, streets were muddy and full of horse manure. No one wanted that in their house.

Meeting Point – Regent Street.

Lower route – Royal York Crescent

The entrances opposite were once used by servants and tradesmen – they were not stables. The stables for these houses were in Princess Victoria Street behind the terrace. These have now become smart mews houses. Towards the middle of the Crescent, note how the road was designed to widen out to allow horse-drawn carriages to turn round more easily. Below you is the private communal garden for the residents of the Crescent. It contains some beautiful trees.

▲ **Royal York Crescent**
Lithograph *c.* 1850
W. L. Walton
(1783-1856)

Meeting Point – Regent Street at the end of the terrace.

This is an opportunity if you wish to explore Royal York Crescent out and back without having to climb steps.

Question 11

Look up at the painted stone carving between Numbers 7 and 8. You can see St George, England's patron saint, riding his horse. What else is he doing?

Upper route – Royal York Crescent

The circular walk continues up the long flight of steps. Climb them and **STOP at the top to admire the vista and to read the following description of the terrace**.

Royal York Crescent description

The original grand design was by William Paty in 1791, who brilliantly matched his building to the natural curve of the hill, using the contours to provide an exclusive stone terrace high above road level, claimed to be the longest terrace in Europe. A financial collapse, caused by the outbreak of war with Revolutionary France in 1793, brought building in Clifton to a halt so that the entire terrace was not finally completed until 1820. It then became a highly desirable place in which to live. Look out at the extraordinary view over Bristol and past the curve of the Paragon and its gardens. Close to you, you will see a plaque on Number 2, *Eugénie House.* It reminds us of the red-headed schoolgirl (*left*) who once reluctantly went to school here. She later became the beautiful Empress Eugénie of France *(1826-1920)* wife of Napoleon III *(1808-1873).*

➔ Walk along the Crescent. Named after Prince Frederick, Duke of York *(1763-1827)* son of King George III *(1738-1820).* He was forced to resign as head of the army when his mistress was discovered to be selling commissions to officers.

Do you remember the song The Grand Old Duke of York? You could sing it as you march along.

The fanlight of Number 4 includes a glass candleholder designed to shed light both inside and out. Each house, including the two levels of basement, has six storeys. Look up at the fine architectural details. Look down at the fascinating courtyard gardens. Look at Number 6. **Question 12**

Outside Number 9, there is part of an unusual advertisement for the company which made the pavement here.

Answer 11

Slaying a dragon. Perhaps it's a Welsh dragon.

How brave!

▲ **Royal York Crescent's elevated path**

Opposite Number 12, you are close enough to see the elaborate floral decoration on the old lamp standard to your right. ● **Question 13** and ● **Question 14**

Number 22 has a beautiful fanlight (another fan-shaped window over the door) and also a plaque giving a brief history of the Crescent. There is a plaque to Earl Roberts *(1832-1914)* at Number 25. He was Commander-in-Chief of the British Army in South Africa during the Boer War of 1899-1902. Continue to Number 39. ● **Question 15**

Reaching the far end, the terrace joins **Regent Street**.

Meeting Point – Royal York Crescent/Regent Street.

Look across Regent Street – the left-hand shop has kept its original nineteenth-century frontage.

There is more to discover on our Clifton walk (refer to map). See elegant buildings that in Edwardian times housed a fashionable store for the rich and discerning. Discover a fine Georgian mansion. Linger in beautiful Church walk. Stop off to visit Clifton's lively Victorian shopping arcade.

● **Question 12**
What does the window over the door of Number 6 remind you of?

● **Question 13**
Look for Number 13. Where is it?

● **Question 14**
Which king's initials are on the red letter box?

● **Question 15**
What can you see on the beams under the balcony of Number 39?

Shortened walk (Refer to map)

If you wish, you could return to the starting point from here – turn left up Regent Street, cross Princess Victoria Street and the pedestrian crossing to Boyces Avenue and the Clifton Village bus stop where your walk began.

Continuing the circular walk.

➔ Cross the road below to take the right-hand pavement of curving **Regent Street**, built in the 1870s and '80s. Look across the road at Number 20 with its attractive crinoline balconies on the first floor. Walk towards the pedestrian crossing and pause this side **just beyond it**. ● **Question 16**

For almost 50 years until 1909 most of these buildings, including part of Merchants Road, formed one of Bristol's earliest and largest department stores, *John Cordeux and Sons,* selling everything from furniture to fashion. Even Cordeux Walking outfits (left) featured in their catalogue. On the top floor 400 seamstresses beavered away making or altering clothes. There were 45 departments employing 300 staff to serve the fashionable customers.The store was the first in Bristol to offer toilet facilities to its lady customers!

➔ Continue along the right-hand pavement. The final buildings opposite, also once part of *Cordeux*, have ornate Corinthian pilasters and carved sea shells over the principal first-floor windows.

➔ Continue to the top of Hensman's Hill. Pause here. This was named after a popular, long-serving vicar, John Hensman (1780-1864) who lived in the house opposite with its pretty chequered brick façade. Dating from the early 1700s it was originally called Cornwallis Grove. From 1959 to 1982 these buildings became part of La Retraite, a Roman Catholic School, and then a retreat and conference centre, Emmaus House.

➔ Cross Regent Street to Saville Place. Walk up the right hand approach, past the 1842 cast iron gatepost, to the houses, leaving the gardens to your left.

Answer 12

A spider's web.

Answer 13

There *isn't* a Number 13. It is supposed to be an unlucky number!

Answer 14

EVIIR
E = Edward
R = Rex (latin for ki
VII = Roman 7
Edward the Seven

▲ **Saville Place**
Begun 1790
Completed in 1838
Charles Dyer, *Architect*

Pause to read on. The houses closest to you, Numbers 1 to 5, are the older houses, begun in the 1790s, but building was delayed following the outbreak of war with Revolutionary France in 1793. It is believed that the original idea was to make a grand terrace promenade at the level of the front doors, similar to that at nearby Royal York Crescent. This never happened, hence the steep steps up to the front doors and the unusually exposed basements below.

At Number 2 there is a plaque to the author Emily Hilda Young *(1880-1949)* who lived here from 1907 to 1918. She wrote several novels about Clifton life in the 1920s and 1930s, thinly disguised as *Upper Radstowe*.

Number 11

➔ Walk left along the terrace. The next houses, Numbers 6 to 11, form a newer part of the terrace which was finally completed by the architect Charles Dyer *(1794-1848)* in 1838. Note the balconies with their bold interlocking scrolls and the fine spear-shaped railings. The vertical design of the fanlights over the front doors is uncommon. ● **Question 17**

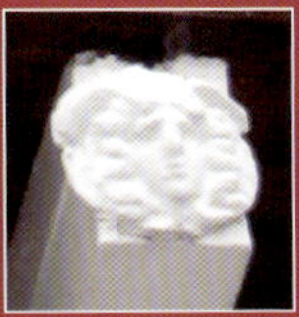

Answer 15

Seven ladies' faces.

● **Question 16**

Look up at the buildings opposite to the right of the zebra crossing. What animals can you see?

● **Question 17**

Look at the metal cover to the coal hole outside No.6. What does the design look like?

Look up at Number 6. The man who designed these houses had his name carved into the wall. Later on someone put a balcony over some of the lettering. What a pity.

Today we have central heating and easy-to-use cookers. A long time ago miners dug coal under parts of Bristol. Coal merchants delivered it in sacks to people's houses by horse and cart. Without coal, families couldn't cook hot food, wash in hot water or heat their rooms. No wonder these houses have so many chimney-pots!

● **Question 18** The last house, Number 11, has an interesting lamp holder for an oil lamp or candle over the door to provide light both inside and out. The *Lime tree* in the communal garden dates from about 1850.

➔ Now walk back to the main road. Go left, keeping to the left-hand pavement of **Clifton Hill**. You will pass a row of houses built in 1901, some with original stained glass.

➔ Walk up the slope. Stop when you reach the entrance to the large mansion on your left. This was formerly *Clifton Court*, built in 1742 for Nehemiah Champion *(1678-1747)*. Champion owned copper and zinc works on the outskirts of Bristol.

Below you, beyond the main road, is a small green – part of the original *Clifton Village Green*. Some claim it derives its name, *Bobbies' Field* or *Green*, from policemen (nicknamed *bobbies*) who trained here in Victorian times. They were so-called after Sir Robert (Bobby) Peel *(1788-1850)* who as Home Secretary established the first police force in London in1829, followed by other cities.

You will pass Georgian *Prospect House* (No.2 Clifton Hill) with its distinctive door and window surrounds. *Beresford House* then follows – both houses were built in 1765.

Answer 16

Bulls.

Answer 17

A flower.

➔ Go through the magnificent wrought-iron gateway of *St Andrew's churchyard.* It supports an impressive lamp. Immediately to your right is the site of the earliest Clifton parish church dating back to 1154. The Methodist John Wesley *(1703-1791)* preached here in 1739. Amongst the graves is that of Ann Yearsley *(1752-1806)* who worked as a local milkmaid when this area was largely farmland, later making her name as the *Milkmaid Poet*. She became the protegée of the philanthropist Hannah More *(1745-1833)*. The War Memorial commemorates Clifton parishioners who died serving their country during the two world wars of 1914-1918 and 1939-1945.

Next, to your right, you will see open ground and low walls, the site of the second, much larger Clifton parish church. This was built in 1822 to meet the needs of a then rapidly expanding population. Sadly, this empty space is all that remains of St Andrew's church, as it was destroyed by enemy action during the Second World War.

▲ **St Andrew's Church**
Built in 1822
Bombed 1940
(Image *c.*1920)

Question 18

Outside Number 8 what creatures decorate the boot scraper?

It is not the church of a poor man, in that atmosphere of eau de colgne, bouquet de la reine, where the glitters of the gilt-edged prayer books and the rustle of brocades present sounds and sights extraordinary to humble comprehension.
Joseph Leech (1815-1893). *The Bristol Churchgoer.*

→ Walk on. To your left you will see a flowerbed planted with *Elizabeth of Glamis* roses. The garden was made by local residents to commemorate the 80th birthday of Queen Elizabeth, the Queen Mother *(1900-2002)*. (Glamis was her Scottish home.) Pause to enjoy the view when you reach this mainly Victorian churchyard.

The beautiful pleached Limes overhang *Church Walk* (often incorrectly called *Birdcage Walk*). The graves here, near the church, are closely packed. The Victorians vied for plots that would bring them *ever closer to God.* ● **Question 19**

The Victorian legacy of mourning trees can still be seen, with black-fruited Cotoneasters and weeping Hollies. Restoring this graveyard has been the Millennium Project of the Clifton and Hotwells Improvement Society. A dedicated band of volunteers has cleared the once overgrown graveyard, planted new trees and shrubs and re-painted the old railings. Note the pretty arched lamp posts.

Wildlife has been encouraged by leaving some areas untended. You may enter the graveyard by one of the gates and there are benches for visitors. It is a peaceful and beautiful area. Please respect the sanctity of this historic resting place.

→ Walk on under the *Lime trees.* You will pass two barley sugar posts. Look right. There is a fountain. The carved inscription in the stonework reads: *The fear of the Lord is a fountain of life.* Prov. The quotation is taken from the Bible – the Book of Proverbs, Chapter 14 Verse 27. Below an ornate shell, carved in stone, you will see a monogram. Who EH was is a mystery. The initials may possibly refer to Elizabeth Hensman, wife of a former vicar of *St Andrew's*, mentioned earlier. The fountain is surrounded by a rope design (suitable for a city with a seagoing history) and there are shell motifs within the small niches below. Notice the eyehook (once there were two), from which would have hung two metal drinking cups. ● **Question 20**

Answer 18

They are sphinxes. A sphinx was an ancient Egyptian creature – half woman and half winged-lion. When this house was built Egyptian things were the latest fashion.

▲**Church Walk**
St Andrew's Churchyard

➔ Cross the road here (called the Fosseway). Pause to enjoy the fine view along the 1845 Lansdown Place opposite. Keeping to the left-hand pavement, walk past the hotel, built in 1865. Cross the main road via the pedestrian refuge to the bollards and enter **Victoria Square** gardens.

This diagonal path is *Birdcage Walk.* The Cut-leaf Beech near the middle of the path and the Tree of Heaven in the far left-hand corner are both part of the original planting of about 1840. On your right is a fine Cedar tree.

Look out for greedy pigeons – and cheeky squirrels running up the trees.

Half-way across look up at the terrace on your right and you will see a stone carving of Queen Victoria's coat of arms. This side of Victoria Square was originally called *Royal Promenade* and dates from 1851.

➔ Leaving the gardens cross the road towards the archway.

Question 19

Look at the really large tomb on your left.
What is special about it?

Question 20

Why are there *two* basins?

Evening on Sion Hill

Answer 19

It is decorated with polished marble and guarded by six angels.

Muffin

Answer 20

The top one held water for people. The bottom one was for dogs.

Look at the last house of the 1874 terrace to your left, Number 15. There is a plaque here to the famous cricketer, Dr W.G. Grace *(1848-1915)*. Just before the arch, to your right, is the attractive detached early Victorian villa, called *Albert Lodge*, named after Prince Albert *(1819-1861)* the Consort of Queen Victoria *(1819-1901)*. The garden boasts some well-clipped topiary and a wonderful *wisteria*.

➔ Go under the arch and walk on into **Boyce's Avenue**. On your right is the Victorian *Clifton Arcade*. You might like to go in. This opened in 1878 as the *Royal Bazaar and Winter Gardens*. Joseph King, the builder, installed a stuffed tiger, fern rockeries, a grotto, a fountain, a restaurant and hired a band to play on Saturdays to attract the crowd. He even kept a cow to provide glasses of foaming fresh milk for his customers. Despite this, the arcade was a flop. It became a dusty warehouse, hidden from public view for many years, until it was successfully restored for shopping in 1992. ● **Question 21**

Albert Lodge

➔ Leaving the arcade, continue to the end of Boyce's Avenue. You are now close to the Clifton Village bus stop from which you began your walk. You may wish to reward yourself with a treat in one of Clifton's many cafés. People living here in Georgian times also enjoyed a good cup of tea.

Looking around, it is not very difficult to imagine the past and the bustle of Clifton life with wealthy Georgian gentlemen wearing powdered wigs and tricorn hats bowling along in their carriages while fashionable ladies, in long panniered dresses and towering hair-dos, strolled by, hoping that their finery would be noticed. Remember too the multitude of less-fortunate servants having to scurry to and fro' on endless household errands, in order to maintain their well-to-do masters' and mistresses' comfortable Clifton lifestyle.

We hope that you enjoyed your walk around Clifton.

● **Question 21**

Strange creatures lurk here – near the roof and over the shop windows. What are they?

The Authors

Julia Killingback

A long-term resident who has been much involved in projects promoting this beautiful area. Julia studied art in Bristol (NDD ATD) designing dress textiles in Paris before returning to Bristol to establish her own Studio. Her designs were used on varied products by well-known companies worldwide. Previous published work. Illustrations for 7 Littlest Poetry Books. Author and Illustrator of 12 children's books (Methuen).

Photographs by James Barke

Michael Pascoe

Michael Pascoe has made a DVD - "Clifton - a place for all seasons" produced by 1st-Take and a book "The Clifton Guide" published by Redcliffe Press as well as writing many articles on Clifton and Hotwells' rich history. More recently, he co-authored the official guide to the Clifton Suspension Bridge. In 2005 he was awarded the Lord Mayor's medal "for services to Bristol and Clifton".

Acknowledgements:

The authors are most grateful for the goodwill and generosity of the following in helping towards the preparation of this book:

Pippa Gibbs for her kind and attentive editing; Simon Bishop for his expertise in graphic design; Richard Bland's assistance with the flora and fauna and Dawn Dyer (Bristol City Reference Library) for her unfailing help.

Our thanks also go to Anthony Beeson, Simon Gibbs, Francis Greenacre, Clara Hudson, Mandy Leivers, Andy Lillie, Tom Mocek, RoseMary Musgrave, Pim Palmen, Maggie Shapland – and Muffin.

The authors would especially like to thank the individuals, families, friends and children who kindly 'route tested' our walks in all winds and weathers – and approved them! Their comments were invaluable.

Answer 21

Dragons – made of metal. Luckily they seem quite friendly.

Credits

The authors and publishers are most grateful for permission to reproduce the following Illustrations which are © copyright of the organisations or individuals listed:

Key

(PC) = Postcard
L = Left – from top down, then base panel L-R
R = Right – from top down, then base panel L-R

Illustrations reproduced by permission of the following:

Bristol Central Reference Library (BCRL)
P9R2; P11R6; P12L4; P26L2; P32L2, L3; P34L2, L3, L5, L6; P36L3; P41R1

Copyright Bristol City Museums, Galleries and Archives (BMAG) P10L1; P19R2(detail); P21R1; P22L5(detail)
The Mary Evans Picture Library
P12L2

The Clifton Suspension Bridge Trust P23R2; P24L4

Avon Gorge and Wildlife Project
Phil Jearey P22L3;
Libby Houston P22 L2

Clifton Rocks Railway
P27R2, R3

John Sansom, Redcliffe Press, Bristol
Back cover image; P6/P7 (private collection) P11R5; P31R1

Kingsmead Press
(now dissolved) P8L5

From Private collections
P4L-R5(PC) P9R3; P17R1 (PC) P19R1; P20L3; P23R1 (PC) P26L1; P37R1

John and Judy Russell P25R3

Alma Martin P41R3

Julia Killingback (Illustrations) P11R3; P14L4; P19R3; P26L5

Front & inside front cover

Simon Bishop

Back cover

Royal York Crescent
Lithograph c,1850. W.L. Walton

Bristol Mayor George Ferguson
Back cover image of Mayor George Ferguson
The Post www.thisisbristol.co.uk

Wallace & Gromit's Grand Appeal
Bristol Children's Hospital Charity
Donate
(www.grandappeal.org.uk/donate)

Every effort has been made to trace and acknowledge the source of all illustrations included. We would like to apologise for any errors or omissions.

Organisations

Avon Gorge and Wildlife Project, The Clifton Club, Clifton Rocks Railway, Clifton Suspension Bridge Trust, The Clifton and Hotwells Improvement Society

Photographs

Most photographs were taken by Julia Killingback and Trevor Palmer. Our thanks are due to Trevor, also to James Barke, Peter Bassett, Simon Bishop, Libby Houston and Gary Thoburn.

Useful web addresses

Avon Gorge and Wildlife Project:
www.avongorge.org.uk

Bristol Central Library:
www.bristol.gov.uk/libraries

Bristol City Museums and Art Galleries:
www.bristol.co.uk/museumsandgalleries

Clifton and Hotwells Improvement Society: www.cliftonhotwells.org.uk

Clifton Suspension Bridge:
www.cliftonbridge.org.uk

Bus information:
www.firstgroup.com/ukbus/bristol_bath

Open Top Bus:
www.citysightseeingbristol.co.uk

Tourist Information:
www.visitbristol.co.uk

Support funding for this project was kindly provided by Bristol City Council Neighbourhood Partnership Well Being Fund

All information is correct at the time of going to press. The authors cannot be held liable for any changes which may have occurred subsequently.

First published 2013
by Julia Killingback
Explorewalks UK

Printed by Short Run Press, Exeter
ISBN 978-1-9064-7781-1

EXPLOREWALKS UK
An imprint of Tangent Books
Web orders:
www.explorewalks.co.uk

For our families with love – and for all who delight in taking a step out of the ordinary
JK & MP

1. CLIFTON

Explore Bristol

EXPLOREWALKS UK

ON FOOT

Other Explorewalks titles in the series

No 2. Victorian Clifton
2013

No 3. Cliftonwood
2014

No 4. Hotwells
2014

For information on other walks guides in this series go to

www.explorewalks.co.uk